THE TRUTH ABOUT THE FOOD SUPPLY™

DAIRY

FROM THE FARM TO YOUR TABLE

BRIAN HANSON-HARDING

fresh

Milk

PASTEURIZED HOMOGENISED
FRESH MILK

rosen publishing's
rosen central®

New York

Published in 2013 by The Rosen Publishing Group, Inc.
29 East 21st Street, New York, NY 10010

Library of Congress Cataloging-in-Publication Data

Hanson-Harding, Brian.
Dairy: from the farm to your table/author, Brian Hanson-Harding.—
1st ed.

   p. cm.—(The truth about the food supply)

Includes bibliographical references and index.
ISBN 978-1-4488-6800-1 (library binding)
1. Dairy farming—Juvenile literature. 2. Dairy farms—Juvenile literature.
3. Dairy products—Juvenile literature. I. Title.
SF239.5.H36 2013
636.2'142—dc23

                                 2011042222

Manufactured in the United States of America

CPSIA Compliance Information: Batch #S12YA: For further information, contact Rosen Publishing, New York,
New York, at 1-800-237-9932.

CONTENTS

W ashington State cherry farmer Helen Reddout was upset. Whenever she and her husband would drive through the nearest town to go to the supermarket, they would have to roll up their windows. The air smelled like a mixture of ammonia, methane, and hydrogen sulfide (which smells like rotten eggs). Reddout would feel like she was going to vomit.

She was smelling a nearby megadairy, which had so many cows that it had a special "manure lagoon" to store all the liquid manure. All over the lower Yakima Valley

On conventional "factory" dairy farms, cows don't graze in pastures but instead eat high-energy feed that is put in front of them all the time.

where she lived, factory dairy farms were opening. Huge barns housed hundreds of cows jammed together standing in puddles of their own urine and manure. Their manure lagoons sometimes leaked, spilling into creeks, roadside ditches, and fragile wetlands. The dairy farmers would spray so much manure over their fields that it wouldn't soak in and would run off into the roads. Flies would swarm by the roads. Smelly, brown clouds would float through the air.

Reddout was personally witnessing a big trend in American dairy farming. Small farms of one hundred cows or fewer were closing and being replaced by huge factory farms. These large dairy farms produce as much milk as possible by breeding large cows that produce a lot of milk, feeding them high-energy feed, and even injecting them with growth hormones.

Milk can be a very healthful food, and Americans consume a lot of it in the form of fluid milk, cheese, butter, ice cream, and other products. Factory farming practices can produce a lot of milk very cheaply, but they can also lead to sick cows, a polluted environment, and milk that may not "do a body good."

This book will describe the different ways milk and dairy products are produced in the United States, as well as the pros and cons for consumers, the environment, and the cows involved.

CHAPTER 1

THE HISTORY OF MILK IN THE UNITED STATES

Americans have been drinking milk for a long time. European colonists brought cows with them beginning in the 1600s. At first, people just drank the milk their own cows produced. Most city dwellers ate cheese and butter but did not drink fresh milk on a regular basis. But over the course of the nineteenth century, more and more Americans got used to drinking fresh milk.

In the early 1800s, dairies began to open in cities. These dairies would be set up near distilleries (which made liquor from grain) or breweries (which made beer from grain). The dairies fed the cows nothing but the "spent" grain that had gone through the distilling or brewing process because it was very cheap. Instead of walking freely through green pastures, these cows were kept confined in dirty pens, where they often developed diseases. Their milk was thin and not very nutritious because the cows lacked the vital nutrients they got from grazing in pastures.

THE MORE, THE BETTER?

Conventional dairy cows produce three or four times the amount of milk they did one hundred years ago. How did that happen? One way was breeding. Dairy farmers would select only breeds that produced the greatest amount of milk—mostly Holsteins. Then they would breed high-producing cows to create even higher-producing cows. To stimulate milk production, farmers would give cows high-energy feed and milk them not just once but twice per day. And finally, beginning in the 1990s, farmers started to give cows an artificial hormone to increase milk production. The synthetic hormone recombinant bovine somatotropin (rBST) is commonly known as recombinant bovine growth hormone (rBGH). It can increase milk production by 10 percent or more, but many people think it can be harmful to humans and cows. According to the U.S. Department of Agriculture (USDA), in 2007, about 17 percent of U.S. cows were treated with rBGH.

Over the last fifty years, the number of U.S. dairy farms has dropped and the ones that are left are getting bigger. Many have more than five hundred cows. Some critics call these factory farms. On a typical large dairy farm, cows spend all their time indoors without much chance to move around. They are fed high-energy feed made from grain and soy to increase milk production. In some cases they are chained up all day, with their heads near a feeding trough. Their rear ends are near a gutter for manure. Farms that work this way are sometimes called confined animal feeding operations, or CAFOs for short.

Cows on conventional farms are often injected with rBST, a growth hormone that increases milk production but can also be harmful to humans and cows.

Some people think this is a good trend. They say that these techniques produce a lot of food very cheaply, producing a steady level of milk. They also say that these techniques are better because they protect animals from weather, dirty conditions, predators, and disease, and they use less land than do farms that let their cows graze on pastures. Huge tanker trucks pull up to these farms and fill up with the milk of hundreds of cows at once, making distribution very easy.

On factory dairy farms, cows live in concrete stalls that are constantly flushed with water, creating a watery mix of manure.

However, because of the crowded living conditions, the feed, the lack of room to move, the problem of cows walking in manure, and the use of growth hormones, it is common for cows to become sick. If one cow gets sick, it is easy for the others to become sick as well. For that reason, these cows are often given antibiotics. In addition to producing a lot of milk in one place, big farms like these produce a lot of something else: manure. Dealing with all this manure takes a lot of work. When the farmers wash out the trenches, the manure becomes liquefied. They store the liquefied manure in holding tanks and later spread it on or inject it into the soil.

THE RISE OF ORGANIC MILK

Many people don't like the way milk is produced on conventional (nonorganic) dairy farms.

FOSSIL FUEL–FREE MILK?

Conventional dairy farming uses a lot of fossil fuel. The grain that cows eat has to be shipped to the dairy farm. Before that, farmers who grew the grain used tractors for tilling, planting, cultivating, and harvesting the grain. They also used chemical fertilizers made from petroleum.

But careful farmers can raise dairy cows almost fossil fuel–free. At Bobolink Farm in New Jersey, the cows eat grass, not grain. So there is no oil used in chemical fertilizers or to run tractors. The cows walk to the pasture instead of having grain trucked to them. And farmer Jonathan White has a really smart way of planting more grass seed. Before the cows go out to pasture, he paints their backs with water and then sprinkles seed on their wet backs. As they graze in the sun, the water dries and the seeds fall off and land on the pasture.

They are concerned about the quality of the milk, the treatment of the cows, and the effects on the environment. For these reasons, organic dairy farming has been growing rapidly since the early 1990s. To have a dairy farm that is certified organic by the USDA, two major things must be organic: the cows and the land. For cows to be organic, they must be fed a diet of 100 percent organic feed. They also must not be treated with prohibited substances,

According to federal law, organic milk must come from cows that graze on pasture a minimum of 120 days or more (depending on location).

like antibiotics or growth hormones. A conventional cow can become organic after one year of this treatment. Starting in 2010, federal law required that organic cows be pastured a minimum of 120 days per year. That means they have to be allowed to roam around on pastures, eating grass and other plants.

Because pastured cows spend a lot of time eating plants that grow from the land, the land must be organic. For land to be organic, a farmer can't use prohibited substances on it, such as chemical fertilizers or pesticides. When the cows graze on the land, they drop their manure on it, too. This manure fertilizes the soil naturally. After three years of this process, conventional farmland can be called organic.

Supporters of organic dairy farming say that organic milk is more healthful, that organic cows are happier and healthier, that organic land is healthier, and that organic farming causes less environmental damage to the water and air. But others say that pasturing cows is inefficient and requires too much land that could be used for other purposes. They also say that organic, pastured cows produce less milk, making organic milk more expensive.

MYTHS AND FACTS

Myth: Cows live peaceful lives, happily munching grass out on the pasture until it's time to come inside to be milked.

Fact: Most cows hardly ever see pasture. Instead, they sit or lie in barns with their heads through metal railings, eating feed out of a trough. The only cows that regularly spend time out on a pasture are the small number on organic dairy farms.

Myth: American cheese is cheese.

Fact: If it's labeled "pasteurized process cheese food," "pasteurized process cheese product," or "pasteurized process cheese spread," it isn't technically cheese.

Myth: Skim milk is the best milk for your health.

Fact: When fat is taken out of milk, so are some of the important vitamins. Furthermore, dairies sometimes put skim milk powder into skim milk to make it seem richer. But studies have shown that skim milk powder has oxidized cholesterol, which can harm your arteries. Finally, skim milk lacks the heart-healthy fatty acids that are present in whole milk from grass-fed cows.

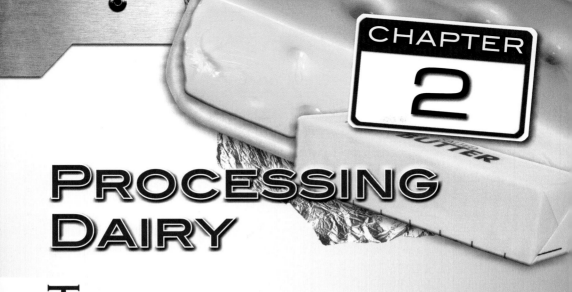

PROCESSING DAIRY

The milk you drink, no matter how fresh it is, is not the way it comes out of the cow. Dairies put it through several processes before putting it in the bottles or cartons you buy in the store. But some people think they're missing out by drinking this processed milk.

THE MILK PROBLEM

In the late 1800s, many people agreed that the United States had a milk problem. The infant death rate was very high, about 50 percent of the birth rate. Many people blamed the high death rate on contaminated milk from the distillery dairies. Finally, two men came up with different solutions.

In the 1890s, Henry Coit, a New Jersey doctor, set up the first medical milk commission. He started the certified milk movement. Certified milk was handled and inspected according to a strict set of rules so that it would be free of germs. Medical milk commissions, made up of doctors, sprang up around the country to certify milk.

Around the same time, Nathan Straus, a wealthy New York businessman, supported pasteurization. Pasteurization is a process in which milk is heated to a certain point to kill germs. Pasteurized milk lasts longer than raw milk before spoiling. That was important because it was hard to keep milk cold. To help the poor people of New York, Straus began setting up "milk depots." They sold low-priced pasteurized milk. By the late 1950s, almost all Americans were drinking pasteurized milk. More and more small dairy farms closed. Large dairies were fewer and farther apart. The larger dairies found it easy to ship pasteurized milk over longer distances.

COOKING OUT THE GERMS

There are a number of ways to pasteurize milk. In Low Temperature, Long Time pasteurization, milk is heated to 145°F (63°C) for thirty minutes. In High Temperature, Short Time treatment, it is pasteurized at 161°F (72°C) for fifteen seconds. Some bacteria survive pasteurization. But they are generally not considered harmful. A few types of surviving bacteria will eventually spoil the milk when it is past its sell-by date. Properly refrigerated pasteurized milk will generally last from twelve to twenty-one days. It should be consumed within two to five days after being opened. Nowadays, a lot of milk and cream is ultra-pasteurized, or heated to 280°F (138°C) for two seconds. Ultra-pasteurized products can stay in a refrigerator from thirty to ninety days before being opened. They are good for seven to ten days after that. However, some people say that ultra-pasteurized milk has a "cooked"

Most milk in the United States is pasteurized. That means it's heated up to kill bacteria.

flavor. Also, it is impossible to make yogurt or cheese from ultra-pasteurized milk because it won't thicken.

DISTRIBUTING THE FAT

Milk was first sold in glass bottles starting in the 1880s. The clear bottles made it easy to see the milk fat. It rose to the top as cream while the skim milk stayed at the bottom. Some people would shake the bottle to mix the fat through the milk. Others would skim off the fat on the top to use as cream. Nowadays, most milk Americans buy is homogenized so that no cream rises to the top. After pasteurization, milk is pressurized and forced through very small holes to break down the fat particles. This way, every glass of milk in a carton tastes the same, from the first to the last.

THE RETURN OF RAW MILK

In recent years, with the growing interest in local foods, an increasing number of small dairy farmers have been producing and selling what is known as "raw milk." Raw milk is not pro-cessed or pasteurized. People who drink raw milk believe that it tastes better and is more healthful. Some worry that pasteuriza-tion destroys or reduces vitamins, kills good bacteria, and makes it harder to absorb minerals from milk. Pasteurized milk is also associated with a number of health problems, including arthritis, heart disease, and milk allergies. Also, some people believe that pasteurization destroys the enzymes you use to digest milk, which puts a strain on your body by requiring it to produce enzymes.

Raw milk supporters say that today's raw milk is produced in much cleaner conditions than it was back when pasteurization was first introduced. In fact, milk that is meant to be sold raw is handled much more carefully than milk that is intended for pasteurization. Some believe that pasteurization is no guarantee of cleanliness and point to *Salmonella* outbreaks that have come from pasteurized milk.

Supporters of raw milk think of it as nature's perfect food, containing vitamins, minerals, enzymes, and fatty acids that are good for you. They think of it as a living food, containing lactic acid–producing bacteria that protect your body from germs. Some argue that substances in raw milk make it easier for your body to absorb vitamins and minerals. They also claim that it has enzymes that help people who usually can't drink milk to digest it more easily.

CONCERNS ABOUT RAW MILK

Many experts, however, warn that drinking raw milk can be dangerous. The U.S. Food and Drug Administration (FDA) advises Americans not to drink

Some people prefer raw, unhomogenized milk. When milk is not homogenized, thick cream rises to the top.

When Milk Came in Bottles

Today, milk comes in waxed paper cartons and plastic jugs. But back in the 1800s, farmers on horse-drawn wagons would deliver milk in buckets. One day, a doctor named Henry Thatcher saw a child's dirty rag doll fall into an open bucket of milk. Then he got the idea to put milk in bottles sealed with waxed paper caps. He called them Thatcher's Common Sense Milk Jars. Soon, most people got their milk delivered in clear glass bottles to their door every morning. When they were done with a bottle of milk, they put the empty bottle outside their door and the milkman would take it the next day. Then the dairy would clean it, refill it with milk, and deliver it again.

raw, unpasteurized milk. The FDA points out that many people have gotten sick from germs in raw milk. According to critics of raw milk, the problem is that a cow's udders are very close to where fecal matter comes from. So it is easy for germs from the manure to get into the milk. Raw milk supporters, however, say that there are no deadly germs in the manure of properly raised, pasture-fed cows.

When Milk Thickens

Cheese starts as milk that is allowed to thicken. Sometimes bacteria or rennin, an enzyme from a calf's stomach, is added. After the milk separates into liquid whey and semisolid curds, the whey is drained off. This remaining part is called fresh or unripened cheese. Some popular varieties include cream cheese, cottage cheese, and ricotta cheese.

To make ripened cheese, these drained curds are cured by one of a number of processes. They may be heated or soaked, or bacteria may be added. After it is cured, the cheese is ripened by being stored, usually uncovered, at specified temperatures. Ripened cheese can range from hard, grating cheese such as Parmesan to soft-ripened cheese like Brie. Some varieties of cheese, like cheddar, are sometimes colored with dye. Blue-veined cheeses are

Cheese is made by allowing milk to thicken and then separating semisolid curds from liquid whey.

injected with mold. Mozzarella cheese is given a hot whey bath and then hand-kneaded. Cheese can be made from pasteurized or raw milk, but the FDA requires raw milk cheese to be aged for at least sixty days.

Butter is made by churning cream, the thickest and fattiest part of the milk. As the cream is beaten, the fat begins to stick together and become butter. The liquid becomes buttermilk. Traditional butter is made from the cream found in whole milk. Commercial butter is made by putting the whey left over from cheese making into a centrifuge to collect the bits of cream that are left.

Butter comes salted and unsalted. By law, butter must have at least 80 percent butterfat.

Yogurt, like sour cream, is basically a form of curdled milk. Bacteria cultures are added to the milk and digest some of the lactose, turning it into lactic acid. This process gives it a creamy texture and a tangy taste.

DAIRY: PERFECT OR POISONOUS?

Many people think that milk is the perfect food. But others think that it can be bad for you. Some people even get sick from consuming dairy products. How can milk be good and bad at the same time?

WHAT'S IN YOUR GLASS OF MILK?

The milk that comes from dairy cows is used for a host of products besides fresh milk: cheese, butter, buttermilk, sour cream, yogurt, ice cream, clotted cream, kefir, condensed milk, and evaporated milk. Powdered skim milk and whey are dairy products that are added to a number of foods. Ninety percent of the milk produced in the United States is grade A milk, which means you can drink it. Grade B milk can only be used to make other products, such as cheese. The milk you buy to drink usually comes in four varieties: whole milk, reduced-fat milk, low-fat milk, and skim milk. Whole milk doesn't have

The USDA recommends three cups of dairy products per day because milk is high in protein, calcium, vitamins A and D, and several B vitamins.

any fat removed, and it contains at least 3.25 percent milk fat. Reduced-fat milk contains 2 percent milk fat. Low-fat milk contains 1 percent milk fat. And skim or nonfat milk contains 0.5 percent milk fat or less. One cup (240 milliliters) of whole milk has 146 calories; one cup of 2 percent milk has 122 calories; one cup of 1 percent milk has 102 calories; and one cup of skim milk has 83 calories.

In ChooseMyPlate.gov, the USDA recommends 3 cups (700 mL) of dairy products per day. Why? Milk provides protein, which builds muscles, and calcium, which builds bones. One cup of milk contains about 300 milligrams of calcium. Milk also contains a number of vitamins, including vitamin A, vitamin D, and several B vitamins, especially thiamin, riboflavin, and vitamin B12. Milk is also a good source of the minerals magnesium, phosphorus, potassium, selenium, and zinc. Some studies also suggest that dairy fights certain cancers and cardiovascular disease, type 2 diabetes, and high blood pressure.

GOING SOUR ON DAIRY

Some people think the USDA puts too much emphasis on dairy products, which can contain a lot of saturated fat. Foods high in saturated fats, such as whole milk, cheese, and butter, can cause heart disease.

artificial flavor, lactic acid, calcium lactate, citric acid, disodium phosphate, annatto extract for color, turmeric oleoresin for color, soy lecithin.

CONTAINS WHEAT, MILK AND SOY INGREDIENTS.

Many people have a hard time digesting lactose, a sugar found in milk. Others are allergic to milk protein.

Many people have a hard time digesting dairy products. Some are lactose-intolerant. Lactose is a sugar present in milk. To digest it, you must have the enzyme lactase. Many people's bodies stop producing lactase after they are small children. For these people, drinking milk, eating ice cream, or consuming other dairy products can lead to discomfort in their stomachs or intestines. However, these people can enjoy certain hard, aged cheeses, such as cheddar, which contain no lactose. Also, yogurt can be easier for them to digest because the bacterial cultures in yogurt produce the enzyme lactase.

Some other people are allergic to milk. For these people, the proteins in milk trigger a bad reaction. The reaction could lead to gastrointestinal symptoms, skin rashes, or coughing and sneezing. Some people with milk allergies can enjoy yogurt. The cultures in yogurt partially digest the milk protein casein, making it less allergenic than milk.

Vitamins A and D are often added to the milk you buy, especially to reduced-fat, low-fat, and nonfat milk. These and other vitamins are fat-soluble. Reducing the fat also reduces the vitamins. Vitamin A helps prevent eye problems, is essential for the growth of cells, and keeps skin healthy. Vitamin D is important because it helps your body absorb calcium. But critics say that one kind of artificial vitamin D can't be absorbed by your body, and another kind is actually harmful. Beside vitamins, dairies sometimes add powdered skim milk to 2 percent milk, 1 percent milk, and nonfat milk to make them seem richer. But powdered skim milk contains oxidized cholesterol, which is harmful to your arteries. So some people argue that it's better to drink whole milk without anything added.

IS IT REALLY CHEESE?

Possibly the most popular cheese product among kids, American cheese is well known for its frequent appearance between slices of bread and on top of burgers. American cheese is usually called processed cheese, which contains cheese and other ingredients such as salt and food coloring. But there are other varieties of American

Some say that American cheese, which contains several other ingredients besides cheese, is not really cheese at all.

"cheese." Pasteurized process cheese must have at least 47 percent fat, while pasteurized process cheese food must be at least 49 percent cheese ingredients and have more than 23 percent fat. There is also pasteurized process cheese spread, which can contain less fat and more moisture. Finally, there is pasteurized process cheese product, for which there are no clear standards.

Consumers like these products because they are smooth, melt easily, and can be stored for a long time without spoiling. Critics of American cheese say it is not real cheese but is made with cheese by-products. There is also concern that these products can be unhealthful because they contain oil, artificial colors, and preservatives.

ICE CREAM: THE DISH OF EMPERORS

The emperors of ancient China were said to be the first to mix snow with sweets to make a frozen treat. In 62 CE, the Roman emperor Nero sent slaves up into the mountains to bring back snow and ice so that his cooks could mix it with nectar, fruit, and honey. Later, when Marco Polo returned to Italy from China, he came back with a new recipe that called for mixing yak milk into snow in order to make it creamy.

Today, ice cream is made by pumping a mixture of milk, cream, sweeteners, and flavorings through a freezer while whipping air into it. Up to half the volume of ice cream is air. According to the USDA, ice cream must contain a minimum of 10 percent milk fat and 6 percent nonfat milk solids. Anything less is merely "frozen dessert." Nowadays, the average American eats about 23 quarts (23 liters) of ice cream every year, according to *Progressive Grocer*, a magazine for the food industry.

WHY GRASS ROCKS!

Many people believe that organic dairy products are much better for you. Organic milk comes from cows that have not been treated with rBGH. A growth hormone, rBGH can lead to higher levels of insulinlike growth factor (IGF-1), which can cause cancer. Recent studies have linked it to different types of cancer. But a number of conventional farmers are also refusing to use rBGH. These dairies say right on the milk carton that no growth hormones were used. Organic milk cannot contain any antibiotics. It also cannot come from a cow that was given antibiotics. If people consume antibiotics in their food, it could make the germs in their bodies resistant to antibiotics. That would make it harder to kill those germs in the future. The FDA does test milk for antibiotics. But the test identifies only a few of the most common antibiotics.

A big reason why many people say that organic milk is good for you is that the cows must be at least partly grass-fed. Milk from grass-fed cows has more vitamins and antioxidants. It also has fewer "bad" fats and more "healthy" fats, such as omega-3 fatty acids and conjugated linoleic acid (CLA). CLA has been shown to prevent heart attacks and possibly cancer. Grass-fed cows produce milk that has higher amounts of beta-carotene, vitamin A, and vitamin E. The real benefit of this milk is based on what the cows eat. "Cows don't make vitamins and nutrients," said Jeff Moyer, farm director for the Rodale Institute in Pennsylvania. "They just transfer it to us. They can't produce what's not in the soil. If we improve the health of the soil, we will have better milk."

10 GREAT QUESTIONS
TO ASK A NUTRITIONIST

1. Is raw milk safe to drink?

2. What should I drink: whole milk, 2 percent milk, 1 percent milk, or skim milk?

3. Is milk from grass-fed cows better than milk from cows that eat grain and soy?

4. What does conjugated linoleic acid (CLA) do for my health?

5. Could there be any bad effects on my health from consuming dairy products from cows treated with antibiotics?

6. Is there anything wrong with drinking milk from cows that have been treated with rBGH?

7. Why is eating yogurt good for my health?

8. If blue cheese is OK to eat, is cheddar cheese that has mold safe to eat?

9. How much butter is all right to eat in a day?

10. Is margarine better for me than butter?

THE COSTS OF INTENSIVE DAIRY FARMING

Modern conventional dairy farming produces a lot of dairy very cheaply. These modern farms use Holsteins, which are very large cows bred to produce a lot of milk. But there is a cost, both to the cows and the environment. Cows that produce a lot of milk often become weak and sick. When conventional farms operate as factory farms, or CAFOs, they often pollute the land, water, and air.

On a CAFO, cows are either in a free stall barn or a set stall barn. In a free stall barn, cows line up in front of a feeding trough, and behind them is a gutter that catches their waste. The gutter is constantly flushed with water. This produces a watery mix of manure. The only time they move is to go to the milking parlor. And when they do move, the cows often walk through liquid manure and stand on wet concrete, both of which can make them lame. In a set stall barn, cows are chained to pipes and milked in the same place they are fed. In both cases, the feed is right in front of the cows all the time. The cows are given high-energy feeds to make them produce more milk. These feeds are made from corn

Cows on factory farms are fed high-protein feed in order to stimulate milk production. But this feed can also make them sick.

and soybeans, which cows don't naturally eat. Eating too much makes them sick. Sometimes, cows are exposed to longer periods of artificial light to make them produce more milk.

THE TOLL ON COWS

Because of the conditions they live in and because they are pushed to produce a lot of milk, cows on conventional farms don't live as long as cows on organic farms do. The average cow lives for a bit over six years. CAFO cows typically live for only three to four years. Cows on organic, grass-fed farms can live for twelve or thirteen years. Bobolink Farm in New Jersey has a cow that is seventeen years old!

Cows on CAFOs are often given rBGH to increase their milk production. When a cow is given rBGH, it creates a lot of stress on its body. The cow produces such a large amount of milk that she loses more nutrients through her milk than she takes in through her feed. As a result, she becomes more susceptible to disease. Also, producing so much milk drains the cows' bones of calcium. This loss of calcium can lead to lameness.

Cows given rBGH are also more likely to have a painful condition called mastitis (inflammation of the udder), cystic ovaries, disorders of the uterus, digestive problems, and lameness. When cows get mastitis, they sometimes pump out bacteria, blood, and pus into their milk. Because of mastitis and other diseases, cows given rBGH are more likely to need antibiotics. Antibiotics in milk can cause health problems in humans. Cows given rBGH have a hard time getting and staying pregnant, and their calves have more birth defects. Finally, giving a cow rBGH can definitely shorten the animal's life. Typically, once a cow is given rBGH, she will live only two more years. In dairies that use rBGH, 40 percent of the cows die every year. For all these reasons, Canada, Japan, Australia, New Zealand, and the European Union don't allow rBGH to be used.

THE TOLL ON THE ENVIRONMENT

The animal waste produced by CAFOs can become a big health and environmental problem. Dairy cows produce so much manure and urine that farmers usually have to store it all in big

On factory farms, liquid manure is stored in lagoons and then sprayed on fields. Sometimes, farmers spray more than the fields can absorb, causing harmful runoff.

lagoons full of liquid manure. The smell can be horrible: like rotten eggs or rancid butter. The decomposing manure in lagoons can give off poisonous gases like hydrogen sulfide, ammonia, or methane. Sometimes, the lagoons burst, leak, or run over whenever there is flooding. In 2005, an upstate New York dairy farm's manure lagoon collapsed. This sent 3,000,000 gallons (11,356,236 liters) of waste into a nearby river, killing 250,000 fish.

Another way of dealing with animal waste is by spraying it on fields. Farmers have always used manure as fertilizer. On grass-fed dairies, cows fertilize the fields as they munch the grass. But the "spray field applications" that CAFOs perform with cow waste often cause problems. The gutters that catch the manure and urine have to be washed with water, resulting in a liquid mixture. This mixture can contain viruses, bacteria, antibiotics, metals, and other harmful compounds. Often, farmers spray much more than the fields can absorb. This leads to runoff that can contaminate waterways and groundwater, which people use for drinking. Also, when the manure is sprayed, it can pollute the air. Studies have shown high levels of sickness in people living near dairy CAFOs.

CAFO manure can contain dangerous pathogens that can be ten to one hundred times more concentrated than what is in human waste. These pathogens include *Listeria*, *E. coli*, and *Salmonella*. CAFO animals are frequently given antibiotics. Some germs can develop resistance to the antibiotics and become "superbugs." CAFO manure could transmit these superbugs to humans.

Finally, conventional dairy farming consumes a lot of fossil fuels to produce the feed for cows and the chemical fertilizers to grow the grain and beans used for feed.

HOW GREEN IS YOUR MILK?

A lot of factors go into producing dairy products in an environmentally sensitive way. If you want to find out how green your dairy is, check out the Cornucopia Institute's Dairy Scorecard (http://www.cornucopia.org/dairysurvey/index.html). Based on answers to the survey questions, the scorecard assigns dairies up to 1,200 points and rates them on a one-cow to five-cow scale.

After grazing all day on pasture, cows head into the barn for milking on an organic dairy farm.

THE ORGANIC ALTERNATIVE

Small pasture-based organic dairy farms are probably best for the environment and the health of the cows. On these farms, cows walk out to the pasture to graze and back to the barn to be milked. They are not fed high-energy feeds that have to be grown with chemicals and fossil fuels. They are not given hormones or antibiotics. They are not pushed to produce more milk than is natural. Their manure is less of a problem because much of it is deposited on the pasture. The dry manure breaks down and enriches the soil, which helps more grass to grow. These farms often use Jersey cows, which are smaller than Holsteins. Jersey cows produce less milk, but the milk is richer in fat. The cows live longer because they are not stressed. They also have fewer problems having calves.

There are also big organic dairy farms that use Holsteins to produce a lot of milk. They feed their cows some grain-based feeds. But the law requires the cows to be out on the pasture for a certain amount of time. So the cows eat a lot more grass and less high-protein feed than cows on conventional farms. That means they require less fossil fuel. Moreover, they are healthier and less stressed. The cows live longer and have fewer problems reproducing.

BEING A SAVVY DAIRY CONSUMER

A popular advertising campaign for the milk industry says that milk "does a body good." Most experts agree that dairy products can be an important part of a healthy diet. But some people are worried about the trend toward big factory farms, the milk they produce, and their effects on cows and the environment.

At the same time that conventional farms are getting bigger, there is a growing demand for organic milk and dairy products. Furthermore, as part of the locavore movement, more and more people are becoming interested in where their dairy comes from.

ASK QUESTIONS

A good consumer asks questions. There are a lot of good questions you can ask about the dairy products you consume. First, were the cows treated with rBGH? For organic cows, the answer will always be no. A package of nonorganic milk will say if the milk comes from cows that were NOT treated with rBGH.

Another question to ask is: does the milk contain skim milk powder? This powder is sometimes added to nonfat or low-fat

From Cows Not Treated with Artificial Growth Hormones (rBST)

FDA says no significant difference has been shown between milk derived from rBST treated and non-treated cows.

Organic milk may not contain any bovine growth hormones, but many conventional dairies produce rBGH-free milk as well, in response to consumer demand.

milk. It contains oxidized cholesterol, which can lead to artery disease. Unfortunately, you won't see it listed separately on the list of ingredients because the law considers it to be milk. But one way to tell if dry milk has been added to fresh milk is to look at the Nutrition Facts label. If the milk contains more than 9 grams (0.32 ounces) of protein per 1-cup (240-mL) serving, you can be pretty sure that dry milk powder was added to it.

Another question to ask is how pasteurized is the milk you buy? Some say that the less milk is cooked, the better it tastes.

If it is ultra-pasteurized, it will say so right on the package. If it says pasteurized, then it was processed by one of the lower-heat methods.

Go Organic, Go Local

A great choice would be to buy organic milk. That way, you know it's rBGH-free. You also know that the cows were eating grass on the pasture for at least one-third of the year. So it will probably have higher levels of omega-3 fatty acids and CLA. If you do buy organic milk, try to buy it locally. You will be supporting local agriculture, plus there will be less chance of it being ultra-pasteurized. Ironically, a lot of organic milk from large organic farms is ultra-pasteurized because it is produced at a central location and shipped to many different places.

Drink Your Cultures!

Yogurt's active cultures—its "good" bacteria—help keep bad bacteria out of your body. It can relieve the symptoms of irritable bowel syndrome as well as prevent yeast infections, urinary tract infections, and osteoporosis. Many eat yogurt for one of these health reasons.

But some people prefer to drink it! In thirteenth-century Asia, Mongol leader Genghis Khan encouraged his warriors to drink *kumis*, a mare's milk yogurt drink, to make them brave. Today, people in the Caucasus region drink *kefir* while people in northern India drink *lassi*, yogurt mixed with water and spices. And some people just put yogurt and fruit in a blender and call it a smoothie!

An easy way to find out how far your milk has traveled is to go to http://www.whereismymilkfrom.com. Just find the five- or six-digit code on your milk container (usually near the sell-by date) and enter it on the Web site, and you'll see exactly where your milk came from.

Finally, you might want to try buying organic milk from local, grass-fed dairies that use Jersey cows. The milk will be richer, and the cows will probably be less stressed than cows on larger organic farms. If possible, visit such a farm to see how the cows are raised.

If you are concerned about the health and environmental issues of milk production, speak up! Let your local supermarket and school cafeteria know that you prefer rBGH-free organic milk or local milk. Write to the FDA and express your concern that it is restricting the labeling of rBGH-free milk.

The best way to send a message is with the money you spend. "Kids vote with their food dollars. If they eat organic food, that's what will be produced. Twelve-year-olds could change the way things are produced," said Jeff Moyer, farm director of the Rodale Institute. "If you ask for organic pizza, you will change the world."

GLOSSARY

antibiotic A chemical substance that destroys bacteria.

antioxidant A substance such as vitamin C or E that removes possibly damaging oxidizing agents in a living organism.

bacteria One-celled organisms that cause disease.

CAFO Confined animal feeding operation, or a factory farm.

cholesterol A substance in the body that gets deposited inside arteries.

conventional Ordinary or typical; in farming, nonorganic.

enzyme A protein in living cells capable of producing certain chemical changes.

groundwater The source of water in springs and wells.

hormone A compound in the body that affects the functions of certain organs or tissues.

lameness The condition of being crippled or disabled in the legs or feet.

organic Grown with the use of fertilizers or pesticides derived from animal or vegetable matter, rather than chemicals.

oxidize To combine with oxygen.

pathogen Any disease-producing agent, such as a virus or bacterium.

pesticide A chemical preparation for destroying pests.

rennin An enzyme from the stomach of a calf used to curdle milk to make cheese.

Salmonella A type of bacteria that may enter the digestive tract of humans in contaminated food and cause abdominal pains and violent diarrhea.

synthetic Relating to compounds formed by a chemical process performed by humans, as opposed to those of natural origin.

FOR MORE INFORMATION

Canadian Organic Growers

323 Chapel Street

Ottawa, ON K1N 7Z2

Canada

(888) 375-7383

Web site: http://www.cog.ca

Canadian Organic Growers is a charitable organization whose mission is to lead local and national communities toward sustainable organic stewardship of land, food, and fiber while respecting nature, upholding social justice, and protecting natural resources.

Health Canada

Address Locator 0900C2

Ottawa, ON K1A 0K9

Canada

(613) 957-2991

Web site: http://www.hc-sc.gc.ca

Health Canada makes policy and recommendations concerning dietary issues. This organization also provides information to citizens to help them make educated decisions about their health.

The Organic Center

P.O. Box 20513

Boulder, CO 80308

(303) 499-1840

Web site: http://www.organiccenter.org

The Organic Center's mission is to conduct credible, evidence-based science on the health and environmental benefits of organic food and farming and to communicate them to the public.

Rodale Institute

611 Siegfriedale Road

Kutztown, PA 19530-9320

(610) 683-1400

Web site: http://www.rodaleinstitute.org

The Rodale Institute is a nonprofit organization dedicated to pioneering organic farming through research and outreach.

U.S. Department of Agriculture (USDA)

1400 Independence Avenue SW

Washington, DC 20250

(202) 720-2791

Web site: http://www.usda.gov

The USDA makes rules concerning farming, and it administers the NOP, or National Organic Program, which sets standards for organic certification. It also oversees ChooseMyPlate, which makes dietary recommendations.

U.S. Food and Drug Administration (FDA)

10903 New Hampshire Avenue

Silver Spring, MD 20993

(888) 463-6332

Web site: http://www.fda.gov

The FDA makes rules about hormones, drugs, and other substances that might appear in food products.

WEB SITES

Due to the changing nature of Internet links, Rosen Publishing has developed an online list of Web sites related to the subject of this book. This site is updated regularly. Please use this link to access the list:

http://www.rosenlinks.com/food/dairy

FOR FURTHER READING

Bliss, John. *Processing Your Food* (Ethics of Food). Mankato, MN: Heinemann-Raintree, 2011.

Cotler, Amy. *The Locavore Way*. North Adams, MA: Storey Publishing, 2009.

Cox, Jeff. *The Organic Food Shopper's Guide*. Hoboken, NJ: John Wiley & Sons, 2008.

DerKazarian, Susan. *Dairy*. New York, NY: Children's Press, 2005.

Harmon, Daniel E. *Fish, Meat, and Poultry: Dangers in the Food Supply* (What's in Your Food? Recipe for Disaster). New York, NY: Rosen Publishing Group, 2008.

Johanson, Paula. *Fake Foods: Fried, Fast, and Processed: The Incredibly Disgusting Story* (Incredibly Disgusting Food). New York, NY: Rosen Publishing Group, 2011.

La Bella, Laura. *Safety and the Food Supply* (In the News). New York, NY: Rosen Publishing Group, 2009.

Pollan, Michael. *The Omnivore's Dilemma: The Secrets Behind What You Eat*. Young Readers' Edition. New York, NY: Dial Books, 2009.

Schlosser, Eric. *Fast Food Nation*. New York, NY: Harper Perennial, 2002.

Schlosser, Eric, and Charles Wilson. *Chew On This. Everything You Don't Want to Know About Fast Food*. New York, NY: Houghton Mifflin, 2007.

Sertori, Trisha. *Dairy Foods*. New York, NY: Marshall Cavendish, 2008.

BIBLIOGRAPHY

Bierman, Edwin L., and Robert E. Shank. "Homogenized Milk and Coronary Artery Disease: Theory, Not Fact." *Journal of the American Medical Association*. Retrieved July 6, 2011 (http://jama.ama-assn.org/ content/234/6/630.extract).

Collins, Karen. "Organic Milk: Are the Benefits Worth the Cost?" MSNBC.com. Retrieved August 1, 2011 (http://www.msnbc.msn.com/ id/14458802/ns/health-diet_and_nutrition/t/organic-milk-are-benefits-worth-cost/ #.Tnt_lXO9z-s).

Fallon, Sally. *Nourishing Traditions*. 2nd ed. Washington, DC: New Trends Publishing, 2001.

Goldstein, Myrna Chandler. *Food and Nutrition Controversies Today*. Westport, CT: Greenwood Press, 2009.

Imhoff, Daniel, ed. *The CAFO Reader*. Berkeley, CA: University of California Press, 2010.

Jonsson, Randall. "Raw-Milk-Facts." Retrieved June 26, 2011 (http://www.raw-milk-facts.com).

Joselit, Jenna Weissman. "Forget Harvey. Got Milk?" *Jewish Daily Forward*, April 17, 2009.

Kirby, David. *Animal Factory*. New York, NY: St. Martin's Press, 2010.

Mangold, George B., Elizabeth Moore, and Minnie D. Weiss. *The Milk Problem in St. Louis*. Department of Research, St. Louis School of Social Economy. Retrieved July 1, 2011 (http://openlibrary.org/books/OL6572873M/ The_milk_problem_in_St._Louis).

McAfee, Mark. "The Truth About Raw Milk with Mark McAfee from Organic Pastures." YouTube. Retrieved June 27, 2011 (http://www.youtube.com/ watch?v=nUG-4uUbjbY&NR=1).

Michaelis, Kristen. "Real Milk." Food Renegade. Retrieved June 27, 2011 (http://www.foodrenegade.com/the-basics/real-milk).

Miller, Deborah A., ed. *Factory Farming*. Detroit, MI: Greenhaven Press, 2010.

Neuman, William. "F.D.A. and Dairy Industry Spar Over Testing of Milk." *New York Times*, January 25, 2011.

O'Brien, Robyn. *The Unhealthy Truth*. New York, NY: Broadway Books, 2009.

O'Hagan, Maureen. "Is Raw, Unpasteurized Milk Safe?" *Seattle Times*.

Retrieved June 29, 2011 (http://seattletimes.nwsource.com/html/local-news/ 2011399591_rawmilk21m.html?prmid=related_stories_section).

The Organic Center. *A Dairy Farm's Footprint: Evaluating the Impacts of Conventional and Organic Farming Systems.* Retrieved September 7, 2011 (http://www.organic-center.org).

Peeples, Lynne. "Is Milk from Grass-fed Cows More Heart-healthy?" Reuters. Retrieved August 8, 2011 (http://www.reuters.com/article/2010/05/28/ us-milk-grass-fed-cows-idUSTRE64R5GY20100528).

"Real Raw Milk Facts." Retrieved June 26, 2011 (http://www.realrawmilk-facts.com).

Robinson, Jo. "Beyond Organic." Eatwild. Retrieved August 8, 2011 (http:// www.eatwild.com/index.html).

Schmid, Ron. *The Untold Story of Milk.* Revised and updated. Washington, DC: New Trends Publishing, 2009.

Shannon, Meg. "How Green Is Organic Milk?" FOXNews.com. Retrieved August 1, 2011 (http://www.foxnews.com/story/0,2933,341950,00. html).

Sustainable Table. "rBGH." 2011. Retrieved September 1, 2011 (http:// www.sustainabletable.org/issues/rbgh).

U.S. Food and Drug Administration. "The Dangers of Raw Milk: Unpasteurized Milk Can Pose a Serious Health Risk." Retrieved June 26, 2011 (http://www.fda.gov/Food/ResourcesForYou/Consumers/ ucm079516.htm).

Valenze, Deborah. *Milk.* New Haven, CT: Yale University Press, 2011.

Weaver, Scott. "Cow Country: The Rise of the CAFO in Idaho." *Boise Weekly*, September 1, 2010. Retrieved September 10, 2011 (http://www. boiseweekly.com/boise/cow-country-the-rise-of-the-cafo-in-idaho/ Content?oid=1755457).

Weston A. Price Foundation. "A Campaign for Real Milk." Retrieved June 26, 2011 (http://www.realmilk.com).

INDEX

A

American cheese, 14, 27
antibiotics, 11, 13, 29, 33, 35, 36

B

Bobolink Farm, New Jersey, 11, 33
butter, 6, 7, 22, 23, 25

C

cheese, 6, 7, 14, 18, 20–22, 23, 25, 26, 27
ChooseMyPlate.gov, recommendations by, 25
Coit, Henry, 15
confined animal feeding operations (CAFOs)/factory farms, 5–6, 8–11, 31–32, 37
    effect on cows, 32–33
    effect on environment, 33–35
Cornucopia Institute's Dairy Scorecard, 35
cream, 16, 18, 22, 23, 28

G

growth hormones, 6, 8, 11, 13, 29, 33, 36, 37, 39, 40

H

Holsteins, 8, 31
homogenized milk, 18

I

ice cream, 6, 23, 26, 28

J

Jersey cows, 36, 40

L

lactose-intolerance, 26
locavore movement, 37

M

medical milk commissions, 15
milk, varieties of
    low-fat milk, 23, 24, 26, 37–38
    reduced-fat milk, 23, 24, 26
    skim/nonfat milk, 14, 18, 23, 24, 26, 37–38
    whole milk, 14, 22, 23–24, 25, 26
milk, vitamins and minerals in, 14, 25, 26, 29
milk allergies, 18, 26
Moyer, Jeff, 29, 40

O

organic milk/dairy farming, 11–13, 14, 29, 36, 37, 39–40

P

pasteurization, 16, 18–19, 20, 22, 38–39

R

raw milk, 16, 18–20, 22
recombinant bovine growth hormone (rBGH), 8, 29, 33, 37, 39, 40

S

skim milk powder, 14, 23, 26, 37–38
sour cream, 22, 23
Straus, Nathan, 16

T

Thatcher, Henry, 20

U

ultrapasteurization, 16–18, 39

Y

yogurt, 18, 22, 23, 26, 39

ABOUT THE AUTHOR

An avid locavore, Brian Hanson-Harding spends much of his free time learning about how his meat, vegetables, and dairy are produced. Aside from maintaining an extensive backyard organic garden, he buys grass-fed beef, lamb, and dairy directly from local farmers and visits the farms whenever possible. A high school English teacher, Hanson-Harding supervises a large and active environmental club that runs the school's recycling program and organic garden, holds cleanups of the local watershed, and educates students about environmental issues. He lives in New Jersey.

PHOTO CREDITS